The Big 3 Management Styles

Paul B. Thornton

First Edition

Multi-Media
Publications Inc.
Oshawa, Ontario

The Big 3 Management Styles
By Paul B. Thornton

Managing Editor:	Kevin Aguanno
Copy Editor:	Susan Andres
Typesetting:	Charles Sin
Cover Design:	Troy O'Brien
eBook Conversion:	Agustina Baid

Published by:
Multi-Media Publications Inc.
Box 58043, Rosslynn RPO, Oshawa, Ontario, Canada, L1J 8L6

http://www.mmpubs.com/

Copyright © 2008 by Multi-Media Publications Inc.

ISBN (Paperback):	978-1-55489-018-7
ISBN (eBook formats):	978-1-55489-017-0

Published in Canada.

CIP Data available from the publisher.

Acknowledgements

While a student at Ohio University, I took Dr. Paul Hersey's course, "Managing Organizational Behavior." His classes were informative, exciting, and full of useful advice. He was a great speaker. You could hear a paperclip drop during his lectures. He quickly became my favorite professor. The Situational Leadership Model developed by Dr. Hersey and Dr. Ken Blanchard is the foundation of my work involving *The Big Three Management Styles*.

Author's Note

The style or approach managers use to engage each employee is critically important. The best managers use a style that fits both the needs of their employees and the situation. Using the appropriate management style provides employees with what they need to be successful. In addition, when managers use the right style, it motivates employees and helps them grow and develop.

Reading this book will help you fine-tune your management styles. You will learn how to apply each management style when performing functions such as communicating, setting goals, coaching, making decisions, and recognizing employees. In addition, you will learn what it takes to transition from managing to leading.

My guarantee—this book will make you a better manager! If you are not 100 percent satisfied, I will provide up to three hours of one-on-one coaching at no charge. My e-mail address is **PThornton@stcc.edu**.

Contents

Management Styles

Management literature describes numerous leadership styles including:

- Assertive
- Autocratic
- Coaching
- Country Club
- Delegating
- Laissez faire
- Participatory
- Team-based

The Big 3 Management Styles

Are there really that many styles? No! I believe there are three
basic styles:

1. Directing
2. Discussing
3. Delegating

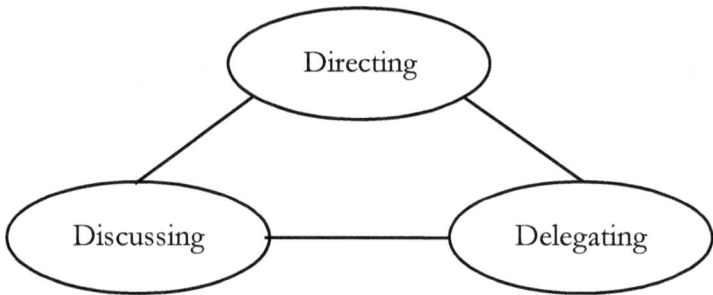

Each style is unique in terms of how managers interact with
their employees.

The Directing Style

The manager tells the employee or a group of employees the following three things:

- What to do

- How it is to be done

- When to have it completed by

The manager assigns roles and responsibilities, sets standards, and defines expectations. The directing style is appropriate when employees lack experience and do not know what to do. It is also appropriate when there is a mandate from senior management that describes *what* must be done and *how* it must be done. The manager is the "Commander-in-Charge," simply carrying out the orders. The directing style is also appropriate in emergencies.

> **An example of the directing style might be the last time you went for a blood test. The lab technician told you to roll up your sleeve and extend your arm. You were shown how to squeeze your hand during the sampling and when to do it. After the blood was drawn, you received specific instructions about holding the cotton swab over the area.**

In some situations, the manager explains why he is taking the action. This is an opportunity for employees to learn the thinking behind the directions.

The Discussing Style

Over 2,000 years ago, Socrates realized that managing and leading were more a matter of asking the right questions than of giving answers. Managers ask focused questions to solicit ideas and opinions from employees regarding the following:

- *What* questions such as what's our goal? What's the problem? What are our options? What's our plan?

- *How* should we proceed?

- *When* does it need to be done by?

- *Who* should do it?

Good questions get people talking and focus their thinking. The discussing style is appropriate when there are opportunities to influence answers to the what, how, when, and who questions. It is effective when employees have ideas and confidence to speak up. Involvement in determining what must be done and how it will be done increases employee commitment to making it happen.

The discussing style can also be used after an employee has completed a task. The right questions force employees to identify lessons learned.

What does a good discussion look like?
Watch Larry King Live. Each night, he has a
discussion with one or more guests. He asks
questions, listens, and probes for more detail
as needed. At times, he digs for the feelings
behind the words. When he has multiple
guests who are simultaneously discussing a
topic, Mr. King strives to give each partici-
pant an equal opportunity to present his/her
points.

Delegating Style

When using the delegating style, managers direct or discuss *what* needs to be accomplished and *when* it must be completed. However, the *how-to-do-it* part of the equation is left up to the employee. It is expected that the employee will take action and make decisions. Employees are given power or authority to make it happen. Managers need to monitor progress at appropriate intervals and take corrective action as needed.

> **An example of the delegating style is when a teacher says to her students, "Your assignment is to research and write a 3-5 page, typewritten paper on 'What are the ingredients of the most effective teams?' Your papers are due October 15." The teacher explains what must be done. How to get it done is left up to each student.**

The delegating style is appropriate when people have the experience, skills, and motivation to get the job done. Experienced employees do not need a manager telling them how to do it. They want freedom to take action and solve problems on their own. The ability to delegate effectively provides managers with more time to spend on other tasks such as benchmarking, strategic planning, and being a more active member in the next level of the organization. Managers can spend more time influencing their boss and peers. It is useful for managers to ask themselves frequently: Am I doing something I could easily delegate to someone else?

Summary

Each management style is unique in terms of how the manager interacts with his/her employees. In essence, managers can

- **Direct**—Tell employees what to do

- **Discuss**—Ask questions and listen

- **Delegate**—Let employees figure it out on their own

Like a good doctor, managers must diagnose the situation before deciding what style to use. Using the appropriate style provides employees with the direction, involvement, support, or freedom they need to be successful. As employees gain experience and become more independent, managers need to move from directing to discussing to delegating.

The Big 3 Management Styles

2

Communicating

E ach management style requires a certain amount of communicating between manager and employees. Communications takes place both one-on-one and in meetings. The ability to send clear messages, ask the right questions, and listen carefully is vital. Each management style emphasizes a particular aspect of the communication process.

Communications—Directing Style

Using the directing style, managers focus on the task that needs to be accomplished. Communications is one-way. The leader speaks; employees listen and react. Managers need to provide specific and precise directions. Employees need to know exactly what needs to be done and by when it must be completed. Communication breakdowns occur when important details are omitted, instructions are vague, or employees do not listen. When giving directions, it is often helpful to start with the big picture and then get into the details. Other points to remember:

1. If possible, show employees the desired output. Take the mystery and guesswork out of what you want.

2. Provide written instructions if the directions are complex or lengthy.

3. Get feedback—test the transfer. Ask the employee to explain in his or her own words what you want done.

How managers deliver the directions and instructions is important. Eric Berne's book, *Games People Play,* helps explain the tone and delivery some managers use. Berne describes the three parts that exist in each of us: the parent, the child, and the adult.

- The child part in us is uninhibited, creative, curious, and impulsive, as well as the one who reacts by whining, rebelling, or acting stubborn.

- The parent in us wants control, order, and stability. The parent can be nurturing and supportive as well as judgmental and controlling. The parent is always right and does not have to explain or justify his/her actions.

- The adult part of us is our mature, rational, problem-solving side. The adult is calm, realistic, logical, and rational but may lack in spontaneity and feelings.

According to Berne, the mature person has a balance of each of the three parts. But some managers take on the role of parent, forcing employees to assume the role of child. The unspoken message from the parent-manager to the subordinate-child is "I'm OK; you're not OK!" I am OK but you need motivation, coaching, direction, or a different job. When managers operate from a parent-child framework, they can come across as being condescending and arrogant.

A healthier relationship between a manager and employee is an adult-to-adult relationship. This relationship produces an "I'm OK; you're OK" attitude. Employees want to be treated as adults. When managers operate from the "I'm OK; you're OK" framework, they are respectful and treat people as equals.

> **Go to www.youtube.org and play Al Pacino's inspirational speech, "Any Given Sunday - Inch by Inch." Observe how he delivers his message and treats each player as an equal.**

Bottom line—when managers give employees direction, it should always be done with care and respect. Treat employees as equals.

Communications—Discussing Style

Managers ask questions that engage employees in discussing their ideas. Two-way communication is the norm. Managers spend as much time asking questions and listening, as they do talking and sharing their ideas.

Effective managers ask genuine questions. Some managers ask rhetorical questions. They use their questions to state their view. "Don't you think it would be a good idea if we..." Genuine questions come from curiosity and the manager's desire to learn. "What do you think we should do?"

Some managers operate from the parent-child mindset. They ask questions more as a test to see if the employee can come up with the right answer. Of course, the manager's answer is the one "correct" answer. I have heard managers ask questions in a way that resemble an interrogation. "Where were you on Sept. 8 between the hours of 8:00 and 10:00 pm?" They ask rapid-fire questions that quickly put the employee on the defensive. The best discussions happen when people are open and relaxed.

In group settings, managers should not allow one or two people to dominate the discussion. Ask questions and get everyone involved. Some managers begin group meetings by saying, "I want to start by giving each of you two minutes to discuss your views on this topic." Managers should withhold their opinion until all employees have had a chance to comment.

Points to Remember when using the Discussing Style

1. Do not use the *discussing* style if you have already made up your mind.

2. Know your objectives. What's the specific purpose of the discussion?

3. Probe and dig. Ask follow-up questions as needed.

4. Observe body language. The non-verbal messages provide important information.

5. Eventually, get specific and assign work and due dates.

Communications—Delegating Style

Effective managers know they cannot do all the work themselves. Being a good delegator is critical. When using the delegating style, mangers may tell the employee what needs to be done and by when it must be done. Or they may discuss what is needed by when. In some cases, those items are left up to the employee. "Jason, I want you to handle the Miller problem." However, in all cases of delegation, the employee determines how to get the work done.

When delegating a task, the manager's tone and delivery is important, as it relates to the confidence she has in her employee. Ineffective managers communicate doubt and questions about the person's abilities to get the job done. "I'm taking a big risk giving you this project." Effective managers do the opposite. "I'm confident you're going to hit a homerun on this project." Once a task is delegated, managers must refrain from giving advice on how to get the task done. Demonstrate enough confidence in your employees to allow them to go to the point of failure if necessary without interfering.

What should managers do when an employee starts asking questions about "*how to get the task done?*" The manager should simply say, "I'm confident you will figure out how to get this done, I want you to decide what to do."

Points to Remember when using the Delegating Style

1. Delegate tasks that challenge people but do not overwhelm them.

2. Do not over-delegate to the same one or two "star" performers.

3. When delegating a long-term project, establish specific follow up dates.

4. Avoid "reverse delegation." Do not allow employees to give back a task that been delegated to them.

5. Never delegate the responsibility for administering discipline.

Summary

Effective managers are clear, concise, and complete in what they say. They treat people as equals-adult to adult-and always show respect. In discussions, they ask focused questions and are interested and curious to learn what employees think. Managers are confident in their employees and communicate that belief when they delegate important tasks.

3

Facilitating the Discussion

A subset of the discussing style is facilitating. The word *facilitate* means, "to make easy." In essence, the manager's role in a one-on-one meeting or in a team setting is to make it easy for employees to participate, follow a logical process, and adhere to the team's rules. Managers who are good facilitators observe what is going on and make interventions that help the individual or team be more productive.

> **Listen to Tom Ashbrook, host of National Public Radio's program *On Point*. He is an excellent facilitator. Note his technique of asking questions, testing assumptions, and making comments that keep the discussion focused and productive.**

Participation Level

In team meetings, the first area the manager/facilitator must address is the level of participation. Who is contributing? Are one or two people dominating the discussion? Are people holding back their true feelings?

Managers can use the following techniques to make sure all team members stay on track and fully participate in the discussion.

- **Ask Questions**—Draw people into the discussion. "Sue, what's your opinion of this option?" "Mike, could you define what you mean by "best-in-class?"

- **Provide Structure**—"Let's go around the table and give everyone a chance to comment."

- **Probe for Feelings and Commitment**—Ask questions that get at the feelings behind the facts. "How do you think the customer would feel about the delay?" "What does our mission statement mean?" Some probes are aimed at uncovering hidden agendas or problems the team has been unwilling to face.

- **Extension Technique**— Ask people to build on the comments made by others. "That's interesting. Could someone add to Joe's comment?" "What would that look like if we were to implement Maria's recommendation?"

Following the Process/Agenda

The second area the manager/facilitator must focus on is the process or agenda the team is following. A common problem teams face is getting off track. For example, what happens at the typical problem solving meeting? Let's assume the problem solving/decision making process involves the following steps:

Step 1—Define the problem

Step 2—Collect and analyze data

Step 3—Generate alternatives

Step 4—Evaluate and select the best alternative

Step 5—Implement

It is common to have various team members focused on different steps. At any given time, one team member may be at Step 1 trying to define the problem, another at Step 3 discussing options, and another at Step 5, having already made his or her choice. Little or no progress is made when each team member is at a different point in the process. Managers need to help the team determine what step they are on and resolve that step before moving onto the next. Equally important, the manager/facilitator needs to make sure the team follows the agenda. When people stay on track and follow a logical process, productivity increases.

Following the Rules

The third area the manager/facilitator helps the team is in following their own rules. Most teams create a few basic rules for members such as:

- One person speaks at a time.

- Attack the issue, not the person.

- Speak up. Say what's on your mind.

- Strive for consensus.

- Meetings will start and end on time.

These rules are established to enhance efficiency and build teamwork. Do team members always follow their own rules? No.

The manager/facilitator can use the following techniques to make sure all team members follow the rules:

- **Ask questions** – Making sure all team members know the rules. "Is everyone aware of the rule regarding listening?" Sometimes, it helps to include the team rules on the meeting agenda or post them on the wall.

- **Determine Commitment** – Making sure team members are committed to the rules. "Is everyone committed to the team rules or should some be changed?"

- **Provide Feedback** – "Your meetings never start or end on time." "Four people were talking at the same time, yet your rule states, 'One person speaks at a time.'"

Summary

Great discussions do not just happen. They require managers who know how to perform the role of facilitator. Facilitators help individuals and team members share their ideas, stay on track, and adhere to the rules. They provide observations and suggestions that help employees become more aware of what they are doing and how they are doing it. Facilitators do not provide all the answers, but rather ask the right questions that help employees learn and become more effective.

The Big 3 Management Styles

Establishing Goals

Managers start the process of setting goals by understanding the organization's overall goals and the specific goals of their boss. The acronym SMART is a useful reminder of the criteria that goals need to have.

- **Specific**—Pinpoint exactly what needs to be accomplished. Vague goals like "improve quality" or "cut costs" are open to wide interpretation.

- **Measurable**—You should be able to measure to what degree you have achieved the goal.

- **Appropriate**—Goals must be set within the context of what's going on in the marketplace. An 8 percent cost reduction may just keep you in the game. A 15 percent reduction may be needed to lead the pack.

- **Results--oriented**—Goals should identify the key deliverables or end results you want to achieve.

- **Time-bounded**—Specific dates and times reduce confusion. Goals without deadlines have a way of slipping away.

Today the business world is very dynamic and fast changing. Managers need to be aware of changing priorities and update goals as required.

Challenging Goals and High Standards

My math teacher set high standards and was very demanding. My English teacher was the opposite. He expected very little from his students. For the most part, student performance matched teacher expectations. The self-fulfilling prophecy maintains, "what you expect is what you get." The best managers establish challenging goals and high standards. They often expect more than others think is possible.

Establishing Goals—Directing Style

The manager establishes goals and assigns them to employees. "Your goal is to sell twelve new cars every month." It may only take a minute to state the goal. It may take several minutes to explain how you want the employee to achieve it. In some situations, managers use the directing style to establish the goal but use the discussing style to strategize how to achieve it.

Employees respond to assigned goals in one of three ways:

1. **Resist**—Employees don't agree with the goals and, therefore, put little to no effort into achieving them.

2. **Comply**—Employees extend minimal effort to achieve the goals.

3. **Commitment**—Employees support the goals and enthusiastically take action to meet or exceed them.

Managers increase the likelihood of getting employee commitment by explaining why the goal is important and what is in it for the employees.

Establishing Goals—Discussing Style

Managers ask questions that draw out employees' ideas and creativity on what the goal should be. "Let's discuss our goals for the offsite meeting." After a productive discussion, specific goals need to be established. The goals may be reached through consensus-both manager and employee agree on the goal. Or goals may be established by the manager after the discussion. If employees are involved in establishing the goals, they are generally more committed to achieving them.

In some cases, managers and employees discuss both what needs to be accomplished (the goal) and how to get it done (the plan) at the same time. However, when dealing with challenging goals, it is more effective and productive to separate the topics. First, discuss what needs to be accomplished, then discuss the plan-how to get it done.

Establishing Goals—Delegating Style

A manager may delegate the task of establishing goals to his employee. "I want you to come up with five-to-seven goals for the next three months. Let's review your goals Friday at 11:00 am." In this case, the employee works by himself to create and establish specific goals. At Friday's meeting, the manager may ask questions and discuss the employee's logic and thinking behind certain goals. The manager may accept the employee's goals as submitted or make changes and additions as required.

Summary

Goals need to be aligned with the company's overall mission, vision, and values. In addition, it is important for managers to understand their boss' goals. There is no one best way to establish goals. Managers should use a management style that fits the needs of the employee and the situation. Established goals should meet the SMART criteria. In addition, it is important to remember that establishing too many goals is as bad as too few.

5

Coaching

Managers coach their employees to perform at their best. Before employees are open to coaching, they need to understand why they need to improve. That is the challenge. That is the need for continuous improvement in all organizations. Secondly, they need to believe they are capable of changing and improving. That is the confidence factor. Coaching involves the "how-to-do-it" part of the equation. It may involve learning a new attitude or acquiring a new skill.

Managers coach by helping employees add, subtract, multiply, and divide.

- **Add** – Managers help employees add new knowledge and skills to their current toolbox. Acquiring new skills such as managing time, running meetings, and using new software help employees become more effective and efficient.

- **Subtract** – Managers help employees eliminate those things that do not add value. Watch great athletes. They have no wasted motions. Managers coach employees to stop doing certain things such as unnecessary paperwork, needless worrying, being a victim, and procrastinating.

- **Multiply** – Managers help employees multiply their strengths and apply them in new ways. For example, a manager might coach an employee to use her networking skills to improve her effectiveness at problem solving.

- **Divide** – Managers help employees divide or separate their tasks into high, medium, and low priorities. In addition, managers teach employees to separate symptoms from underlying problems, facts from opinions, effort from results, and what has to be done from how difficult it is to get it done.

As you can see, coaching does not always involve adding new skills. It often involves stopping self-defeating behaviors and applying strengths in new ways.

Giving Feedback

An important aspect of coaching involves giving feedback.
Before giving feedback, managers need to spend time observ-
ing an employee's current performance. What is the quality
and quantity of his work? What are his top priorities? What
knowledge and skills does the person possess? What is his
level of motivation?

- Be specific

- Build on strengths

- Focus on one or two improvement opportunities

- Gain employee commitment

Coaching—Directing Style

The manager tells the employee one or more of the following:

- What to do

- How to do it

- What to eliminate or stop doing

In some situations, the manager demonstrates how to do a
particular task.

Using the directing style, the manager coaches and
provides feedback by telling the person what he is doing right
and what he is doing wrong. He specifies what changes need to
be made, providing candid and detailed instructions. In some
cases, the manager tells the employee what he wants him to do
more of and/or less of. "In meetings, I want you to be less
quiet and more assertive in stating your views."

Coaching—Discussing Style

Managers ask questions that directly involve the employee in examining his or her own performance and identifying behaviors that are more effective. "Joe, what's your critique of how you ran yesterday's meeting with our field service representatives?" In this example, Joe is diagnosing his strengths and opportunities for improvement. The next step is discussing ideas and actions Joe could take to increase his effectiveness.

The manager asks questions such as the following:

- What went well?

- What would you change next time?

- What did you learn?

- What are the keys to…

- Have you considered…

- What was the consequence of what you did?

- How will you know when/if…

In some situations, managers use active listening to mirror back what the employee is saying. This approach helps the employee come to his own insights about what is working and not working.

Coaching—Delegating Style

Using the delegating style, the manager might say something such as the following, "I want you to think about your performance on this assignment. Identify three things you did well and one area needing improvement. I'd like to meet tomorrow at 10:00 am to hear what you come up with." In essence, the manager is having the employee do self-coaching. Part of an employee's growth and development is gaining the ability to critique his own performance.

Observe examples of each coaching style by watching the following movies:

- *Dead Poet's Society*

- *Akeelah and the Bee*

- *Pay It Forward*

- *Hoosiers*

- *Tuesdays with Morrie*

Points to Remember about Coaching

1. Take advantage of "teachable moments"—times when people are most open to receiving feedback.

2. Describe current performance. Be prepared to provide one or more specific examples.

3. Explain the business consequences of current performance. Late deliveries? Upset customers? Poor quality? Unhappy employees? It is very important for people to understand the full consequences of their behavior.

4. Show the employee what good or great performance looks like.

5. Make or discuss specific suggestions on how to improve.

6. Do not over coach.

Summary

The best coaching action may be demonstrating what to do, providing feedback, asking a question, calling a timeout for reflection, or doing nothing. Managers believe in people's potential to improve. Top managers help employees focus on what is important, gain new skills, and eliminate things that do not add value. Using the appropriate coaching style helps employees become more self aware and responsible for diagnosing their own performance.

Problem Solving / Decision Making

A problem exists when there is a gap between "what is happening" versus "what should be happening."

Fast-paced competition continues to shorten the time managers have to define and solve problems. Some decisions are routine, such as ordering parts and scheduling vacations. However, 10 percent to 20 percent of the decisions managers make require thoughtful attention to each step in the problem solving/decision making process.

Three important questions managers need to ask when confronted with a problem include

- Who owns the problem? (Just because you are presented with a problem does not necessarily mean it is yours to solve.)

- How much time, effort, and money should go into solving the problem? (Not all problems are equal in importance.)

- What approach should be used to address the problem? Should it be assigned to an individual? A team? Should an external consultant be hired?

The steps involved in the problem solving/decision making process include:

1. Define the problem. Separate symptoms from underlying problems. Ask "why" multiple times until you get to the root cause of the problem.

2. Identify possible solutions. There is always more than one option. Do research and find out how others have solved similar problems. Brainstorm.

3. Evaluate options. Do a cost/benefit analysis of each option.

4. Select the best option—make a decision.

Problem Solving/ Decision Making— Directing Style

The manager defines the problem, evaluates options, and makes a decision. Next, the manager tells the employee what he wants done. The directing approach allows for quick decisions when time is critical. If the building were on fire, you would not want your manager to call a meeting to brainstorm options. You want someone to take charge and make quick decisions.

Managers often do not have all the facts and information they would like to have before making a decision. They must make decisions based on a combination of the "facts" and "gut feel."

Problem Solving/Decision Making— Discussing Style

Both the manager and employee play an active role in each of the steps of the problem solving/decision making process. "How do you see the problem?" "What options make sense to you?" Of course, this approach takes more time. But, employee involvement generates more ideas and generally more commitment to the eventual decision.

> Watch the TV show *The Apprentice*. At the end of each week's episode, Donald Trump decides who should be fired from the losing team. Trump asks questions and listens to several people including the losing team leader, members of the losing team, and his staff who have directly observed the team. Once he has all the inputs, he makes a decision and utters the words, "You're fired."

Problem Solving/Decision Making— Delegating Style

The manager gives one or more employees the responsibilities and authority to make decisions. In this situation, the employee by himself makes the decision. Managers need to give a deadline as to by when the decision must be made. "Fred, by next Tuesday you need to give me your decision on the open requisitions."

Points to Remember about Decision Making

1. Managers seldom have have all the information they would like but still need to make a decision.

2. There is always more than one option.

3. Be decisive. There are situations when it is best to make a decision and ask for forgiveness later.

4. Sometimes managers need to make unpopular decisions.

Summary

Every day, managers deal with a variety of problems. Many are routine and simple. But a few are complex and very impactful. The first thing managers must decide is-who owns the problem? If the manager owns the problem, he must determine priority and decide what style of management to use in solving it. The best managers adapt their approach to problem solving/decision making to meet the needs of their employees and the challenges they face.

Rewarding and Recognizing

E ffective managers reward and recognize employees for good or improved performance. Author and consultant Ken Blanchard coined the phrase, "Catch them doing something right." When managers recognize people, they are really saying, "I've noticed." For example, the manager may have noticed "better quality," "lower cost," "improved teamwork," "faster response time," and so on. Employees want to be noticed and to feel appreciated. It is also important to recognize or acknowledge employee "effort." Many employees are working ten-to-twelve-hour days. This type of effort deserves recognition.

Some of the important points to keep in mind when recognizing employees include

- The recognition/reward should be appropriate for what the employee did

- Be timely. The sooner you praise the employee, the better.

- Be specific.

Recognition is often followed by a reward such as

- A pay increase

- Movie tickets

- Time off

- Diner for two

Rewarding and Recognizing— Directing Style

The manager praises the employee for following directions and doing exactly what he was told to do. "Great job! You did it exactly as I wanted."

Rewarding and Recognizing— Discussing Style

The manager has an open discussion so all team members have an opportunity to recognize the contributions of a team member. In some cases, the recognition involves a discussion about the positive comments a customer, supplier, or competitor has said about an employee.

Rewarding and Recognizing— Delegating Style

After the completion of a major accomplishment, the manager may want to delegate the recognizing/rewarding event to his boss or a senior manager (VP or president). When the president of the company does the recognition, it generally has more impact.

Points to remember about Rewarding and Recognizing

1. Reward and recognize employees for responding appropriately (following directions, providing input, and working independently) to the management style being used

2. Recognize and reward employees for both effort and results

3. Build people up; do not tear them down

Summary

The best managers look for opportunities to reward and recognize employees for both effort and results. They do it in small ways, one-on-one interactions, as well as in public forums such as department meetings.

The Big 3 Management Styles

Leading

What is the difference between managing and leading? Managers use current methods, procedures, and resources to get the job done. Leaders are more focused on change. They want to pursue a new vision. They want to change the organization's mission, values, structure, strategy, and/or processes.

Management styles become leadership styles when the focus is on helping people change and pursue a new vision.

Leading—Directing Style

Leaders tell employees they must change. They explain why change is needed and what will be done to make it happen.

As part of the change effort, leaders often establish demanding goals. These demands force employees to rethink what they do and how they do it. Various CEOs have described these goals as "stretch goals" or "killer goals."

A stretch goal is one that is significantly outside an employee's comfort zone; therefore, the person or team has no idea of how to achieve it. For example, "Cut cycle time from six weeks to three days," "Reduce cost by 35 percent," "Increase market share from 8 percent to 28 percent." In these situations, the leader devises radically different ways of working. To achieve a stretch goal, you cannot just work harder, you must work much smarter and differently. Using the directing style, leaders tell employees what the big goal is and what must be done to achieve it.

> **Watch the movie *Remember the Titans*.**
> **Observe the directing leadership style Coach**
> **Boone uses to integrate the two groups of**
> **high school football players.**

In essence, the leader forces the employees to change or suffer the consequences. The directing approach mows over any resistance from employees.

Leading—Discussing Style

Leaders ask big provocative questions such as those listed below. These questions force employees to rethink their mission and strategies.

1. "What today is impossible to do but would fundamentally change your business?" (Joel Barker)

2. "What great thing in life would you attempt if you knew it was impossible to fail?" (Dr. Robert Schuller)

3. "If we were not already in this business, would we go into it now?" (Peter Drucker)

In a *Harvard Business Review* article entitled "The Work of Leadership," Ronald Heifetz and Donald Laurie make it clear that today's leaders do not provide all the answers. Instead, leaders ask tough questions. Leaders challenge "the way business is being conducted." Involving employees in the change process helps reduce employee resistance to change. In addition, employee input generates useful information that helps in designing the change and implementation strategies.

Leading—Delegating Style

In some cases, leaders require employees to discover for themselves that change is needed.

Leaders create opportunities for employees to experience excellence or observe top performance. Employees discover for themselves what is possible and what changes are needed. For example, at one company, unionized hourly employees were unwilling and unmotivated to make step change improvements in productivity and quality. The plant manager arranged to have the employees visit a best-in-class company and see what was possible. Seeing is believing! Employees discovered a significant gap in their performance and what was possible. That gap became a challenge and motivational force to improve and become the market leader.

Once employees understand the need for change, leaders delegate to them the responsibility actually to design and implement the needed changes.

> **Check out these blogs for ongoing education about effective leadership:**
>
> - *Leading Blog - Building Community Leaders* by **Michael McKinney**
>
> - *Leadership Turn* by **Jonathan Farrington**
>
> - *Extreme Leadership* by **Steve Farber**
>
> - *Dispatches from the New World of Work* by **Tom Peters**
>
> - *Mick's Leadership Blog* by **Mick Yates**

Points to Remember about Leading

1. Leaders explain why change is needed.

2. They inspire people to change.

3. They provide education and training to help employees change.

4. Early success builds momentum for continued change

Summary

Managers become leaders when they focus on big changes. Leaders use a leadership style that helps employees see the need for change and understand the benefits it will derive. In essence, leaders see what is possible, describe what is possible, and pursue what is possible. They not only get people to buy into their vision, but also take steps to implement the change.

The Big 3 Management Styles

9

Managing your Bosses and Peers

It is important for managers to have a positive working relationship with their bosses and peers. Bosses influence and control the resources (people, budget, equipment etc.) managers get to do their job. Peers can provide suggestions and support in helping managers accomplish their goals. There are times when managers use each of the styles when dealing with bosses and peers.

- **Directing style**—Telling your boss what to do takes courage. Many managers are afraid and unwilling to speak up to their boss or peers. They are "yes people," always agreeing with the boss. The best managers and leaders are willing to speak up, make waves, and challenge their boss and peers when necessary.

- **Discussing style**—This style is the one managers use most frequently. They ask questions of their boss and peers for one or more of the following:

  ★ Ask for resources-people, equipment, money, etc.

  ★ Solicit advice and guidance.

  ★ Plant seeds for them to consider new ideas.

  ★ Ask for support and commitment.

  Managers need to prepare for these interactions by making sure their questions are focused and clear.

- **Delegating style**—This style is appropriate in certain cases. However, when delegating to your boss or a peer, you ask him or her to take on a task. "Jason, are you willing to take on the leadership of the mentor program?" The manager needs to be able to explain why he needs help from his boss or peer.

When managers deal with their boss and peers, they are trying to influence them to think a certain way or take a specific action. Influential managers are good at stating the business case as to what should be done and why it is needed. They are also good at bargaining. "If you will do 'X' for me, I'll do 'Y' for you." In addition, managers are also good at networking. They have a strong professional circle to acquire information, get advice, and obtain assistance from others.

Being influential often starts with understanding the needs and goals of those you are trying to influence. Managers tie the benefits of their ideas into the needs of others. "Here is my proposal and here is how it will help you accomplish your goals." In addition, just as the best sales reps, managers are willing to ask for the sale, "Will you support my proposal at today's meeting?"

Summary

Managers use an appropriate management style to gain help and support from their boss and peers.

10

Summary of the 3 Management Styles

Some of the important points to remember include

- There is no one best style of management. Each style is appropriate and useful in certain circumstances.

- Every workday, there are opportunities to use each of the three management styles.

- As employees grow, develop, and gain experience, managers need to move from directing to discussing to delegating.

- The directing style requires managers to be effective at sending clear, concise, and complete messages.

- The discussing style requires managers to be effective at asking focused questions and listening.

- The delegating style requires managers to be effective at letting go and giving employees the freedom to do it "their way."

- Do not micromanage.

- Managers should show respect and operate from an adult-to-adult framework whenever they communicate with employees.

- Goals should have the SMART characteristics.

- Coaching does not always involve adding new skills. It may involve determining what the employee should stop doing or how to use their strengths in new ways.

- Management styles become leadership styles when the focus is on major change.

- Leaders see what is possible, describe what is possible, and pursue what is possible. They inspire people to change.

- Perfecting your management and leadership skills is a life-long journey.

Bibliography

Beck, John, and Neil Yeager. *The Leader's Window: Mastering the Four Styles of Leadership to Build High Performing Teams.* 1ˢᵗ ed. New York: John Wiley & Son, 1994.

Blanchard, Ken, and the founding associates and consulting partners of the Ken Blanchard Companies. *Leading at a Higher Level.* 1ˢᵗ ed. New Jersey: Pearson/Prentice Hall, 2006.

Heifetz, Ronald A., and Donald L. Laurie. "The Work of Leadership." *Harvard Business Review.* January-February (1979).

Hersey, Paul. *The Situational Leader.* 1ˢᵗ ed. Escondido, CA: The Center for Leadership Studies, 1985.

Hersey, Paul, and Ken Blanchard. *Management of Organizational Behavior.* 4ᵗʰ ed. Englewood Cliffs, NJ: Prentice Hall, 1982.

Jones, Laurie B. *Jesus CEO: Using Ancient Wisdom for Visionary Leadership.* 1ˢᵗ ed. New York: Hyperion, 1995.

Kaplan, Robert E., and Rob Kaiser. "Developing versatile leaders." *MIT Sloan Management Review.* Summer (2003).

Kotter, John. *Leading Change.* 1ˢᵗ ed. Cambridge, MA: Harvard University Press, 1996.

Kouzes, Jim, and Barry Posner. *The Leadership Challenge*. 2nd ed. San Francisco, CA: Jossey-Bass Publishers, 1995.

Ludeman, Kate, and Eddie Erlandson. "Coaching the Alpha Male." *Harvard Business Review*. May (2004).

Samiec, Ellen, and Scott Campbell. "You Can't Win at Golf with One Club: Effective Leaders Excel in Five Dimensions." *Leadership Excellence*. March (2006).

Shechtman, Morris R. *Working Without a Net: How to Survive and Thrive in Today's High Risk Business World*. 1st ed. New York: Pocket Books, 1994.

Thornton, Paul B. *Be the Leader, Make the Difference*. 1st ed. Torrance, CA: Griffin Publishing Group, 2000.

Thornton, Paul B. "Teamwork: Focus, Frame, Facilitate." *Management Review*. November (1992).

Tichy, Noel M., with Eli Cohen. *The Leadership Engine*. 1st ed. New York: HarperCollins Publishers, 1997.

Other Research

Interviews, discussions, blogs, seminars, and teleforums with various authors, consultants, managers, and leaders:

- Warren Bennis, Distinguished Professor of Business Administration and Founding Chairman of The Leadership Institute at the University of Southern California

- Ruth Branson, Senior Vice President, Human Resources, Shaw's Supermarkets

- Tricia Day, Chief Labor Relations Officer, Massachusetts Bay Transportation Authority

- Janice Deskus, Vice President, Training and Quality Implementation, CIGNA Health Care

- Marshall Goldsmith, Executive Coach

- Michael Z. Kay, President and CEO, LSG Sky Chefs, Inc.

- Dan Kelly, Vice President, Transportation Business, International Fuel Cells

- Ayn LaPlant, President and CEO, Beekley Corporation

- Sue Lewis, Executive Vice President and Chief Real Estate Officer, The Travelers

- Michael Niziolek, Vice President, Human Resources, Hasbro Games

- Tom Peters, author and consultant

- Tony Schwartz, co-author of *The Power of Full Engagement*

- Roger Schwarz, President, Roger Schwarz & Associates

- Mary Jean Thornton, college professor, former executive, and small business owner

- Patricia Wheeler, executive coach

About the Author

Paul B. Thornton is a speaker, author, coach, and professor of business administration at Springfield Technical Community College. He also is an associate professor at large for the Thierry Graduate School of Leadership located in Brussels, Belgium.

Thornton, president of Be the Leader Associates, has designed and conducted management/ leadership programs for several companies, including Mercy Health Systems, Palmer Foundry, UMASS Medical School, Management Development International, Kuwait Oil Corporation, Young Presidents Organization, and United Technologies Corporation. His most popular seminars include

- Situational Management Styles

- Be the Leader, Make the Difference

- Dealing with Difficult People

He is the author of twelve books on management and leadership and numerous articles. His book *Be the Leader, Make the Difference* was selected as "one of the best business books of all time" by The CEO Refresher web site. Executive coach Marshall Goldsmith said, "Paul Thornton's book, *Best Leadership Advice I Ever Got*, contains some of the best coaching on leadership that you will ever receive."

His email address is PThornton@stcc.edu.

Did you like this book?

If you enjoyed this book, you will find more interesting books at

www.MMPubs.com

Please take the time to let us know how you liked this book. Even short reviews of 2-3 sentences can be helpful and may be used in our marketing materials. If you take the time to post a review for this book on Amazon.com, let us know when the review is posted and you will receive a free audiobook or ebook from our catalog. Simply email the link to the review once it is live on Amazon.com, with your name, and your mailing address—send the email to orders@mmpubs.com with the subject line "Book Review Posted on Amazon."

If you have questions about this book, our customer loyalty program, or our review rewards program, please contact us at info@mmpubs.com.

Multi-Media Publications Inc.

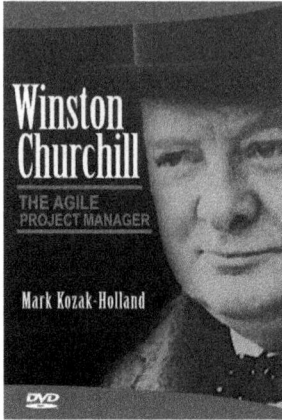

Winston Churchill: The Agile Project Manager

Today's pace of change has reached unprecedented levels only seen in times of war. As a result, project management has changed accordingly with the pressure to deliver and make things count quickly. This recording looks back at a period of incredible change and mines lessons for Project Managers today.

In May 1940, the United Kingdom (UK) was facing a dire situation, an imminent invasion. As the evacuation of Dunkirk unfolded, the scale of the disaster became apparent. The army abandoned 90% of its equipment, the RAF fighter losses were deplorable, and over 200 ships were lost.

Winston Churchill, one of the greatest leaders of the 20th century, was swept into power. With depleted forces and no organized defense, the situation required a near miracle. Churchill had to mobilize quickly and act with agility to assemble a defense. He had to make the right investment choices, deploy resources, and deliver a complete project in a fraction of the time. This recording looks at Churchill as an agile Project Manger, turning a disastrous situation into an unexpected victory.

ISBN: 1-895186-50-1   (Audio CD)
ISBN: 1-897326-38-6   (DVD)

http://www.PM-Audiobooks.com

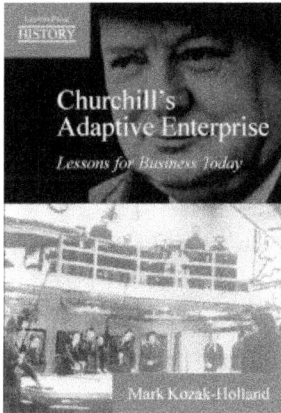

Churchill's Adaptive Enterprise: Lessons for Business Today

This book analyzes a period of time from World War II when Winston Churchill, one of history's most famous leaders, faced near defeat for the British in the face of sustained German attacks. The book describes the strategies he used to overcome incredible odds and turn the tide on the impending invasion. The historical analysis is done through a modern business and information technology lens, describing Churchill's actions and strategy using modern business tools and techniques. Aimed at business executives, IT managers, and project managers, the book extracts learnings from Churchill's experiences that can be applied to business problems today. Particular themes in the book are knowledge management, information portals, adaptive enterprises, and organizational agility.

Eric Hoffer Book Award (2007) Winner

ISBN: 1-895186-19-6   (paperback)
ISBN: 1-895186-20-X   (PDF ebook)

http://www.mmpubs.com/churchill

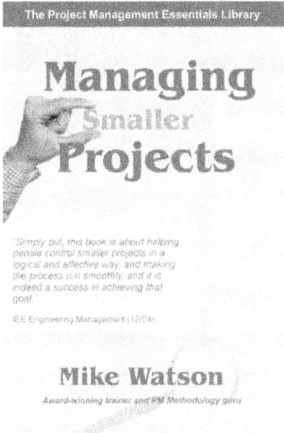

Managing Smaller Projects: A Practical Approach

So called "small projects" can have potentially alarming consequences if they go wrong, but their control is often left to chance. The solution is to adapt tried and tested project management techniques.

This book provides a low overhead, highly practical way of looking after small projects. It covers all the essential skills: from project start-up, to managing risk, quality and change, through to controlling the project with a simple control system. It cuts through the jargon of project management and provides a framework that is as useful to those lacking formal training, as it is to those who are skilled project managers and want to control smaller projects without the burden of bureaucracy.

Read this best-selling book from the U.K., now making its North American debut. *IEE Engineering Management* praises the book, noting that "Simply put, this book is about helping people control smaller projects in a logical and effective way, and making the process run smoothly, and is indeed a success in achieving that goal."

Available in print format. Order from your local bookseller, Amazon.com, or directly from the publisher at
www.mmpubs.com/msp

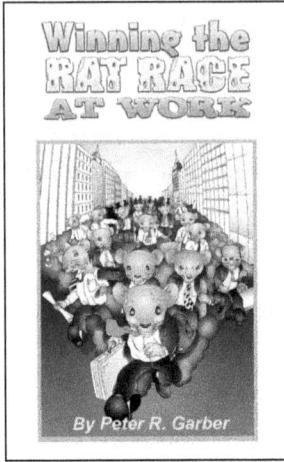

Want to Get Ahead in Your Career?

Do you find yourself challenged by office politics, bad things happen-ing to good careers, dealing with the "big cheeses" at work, the need for effective networking skills, and keeping good working relation-ships with coworkers and bosses? *Winning the Rat Race at Work* is a unique book that provides you with case studies, interactive exercises, self-assessments, strategies, evaluations, and models for overcom-ing these workplace challenges. The book illustrates the stages of a career and the career choices that determine your future, empowering you to make positive changes.

Written by Peter R. Garber, the author of *100 Ways to Get on the Wrong Side of Your Boss*, this book is a must read for anyone interested in getting ahead in his or her career. You will want to keep a copy in your top desk drawer for ready reference whenever you find yourself in a challenging predica-ment at work.

ISBN: 1-895186-68-4   (paperback)
Also available in ebook formats. Order from your local bookseller, Amazon.com, or directly from the publisher at
http://www.mmpubs.com/rats

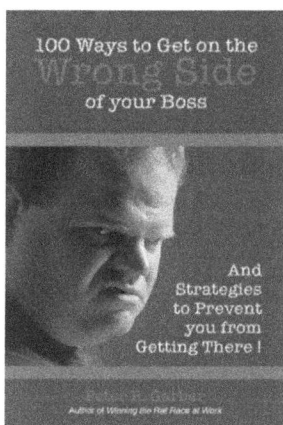

100 Ways to Get on the
Wrong Side
of your Boss

And
Strategies
to Prevent
you from
Getting There !

Author of Winning the Rat Race at Work

Need More Help with the Politics at Work?

100 Ways To Get On The Wrong Side Of Your Boss (And Strategies to Prevent You from Getting There!) was written for anyone who has ever been frustrated by his or her working relationship with the boss—and who hasn't ever felt this way! Bosses play a critically important role in your career success and getting on the wrong side of this important individual in your working life is not a good thing.

Each of these 100 Ways is designed to illustrate a particular problem that you may encounter when dealing with your boss and then an effective strategy to prevent this problem from reoccurring. You will learn how to deal more effectively with your boss in this fun and practical book filled with invaluable advice that can be utilized every day at work.

Written by Peter R. Garber, the author of *Winning the Rat Race at Work*, this book is a must read for anyone interested in getting ahead. You will want to keep a copy in your top desk drawer for ready reference whenever you find yourself in a challenging predicament at work.

ISBN: 1-895186-98-6   (paperback)
Also available in ebook formats. Order from your local bookseller, Amazon.com, or directly from the publisher at **http://www.InTroubleAtWork.com**

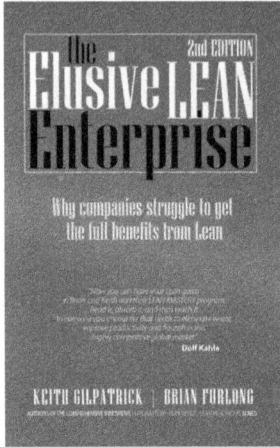

The Elusive Lean Enterprise: Why Companies Struggle to Get the Full Benefits from Lean

In today's fast-paced and volatile business environment, customers are demanding increased flexibility and lower cost, and companies must operate in a waste-free environment to maintain a competitive edge and grow margins. Lean Enterprise is the process that companies are adopting to provide superior customer service and improve bottom line performance.

Are you contemplating Lean Enterprise for your manufacturing or office facility? Are you already implementing Lean, but dissatisfied with the speed of change? Do your employees think that Lean is just the new flavor of the month? Are you being forced to go Lean by your customers? This book is designed to help guide you through the Lean transformation and avoid the pitfalls. Find out why many companies are failing to live up to the promise of Lean, and why there may be alternatives to outsourcing or going offshore.

ISBN: 1-897326-64-5   (paperback)
ISBN: 1-897326-65-3   (hardcover)
ISBN: 1-897326-66-1   (Adobe PDF ebook)

Order from your local bookseller, Amazon.com, or directly from the publisher at **http://www.mmpubs.com**

Networking *for* Results

In partnership with Michael J. Hughes, *The* Networking Guru, Multi-Media Publications Inc. has released a new series of books, ebooks, and audio books designed for business and sales professionals who want to get the most out of their networking events and help their career development.

Networking refers to the concept that each of us has a group or "network" of friends, associates and contacts as part of our on-going human activity that we can use to achieve certain objectives.

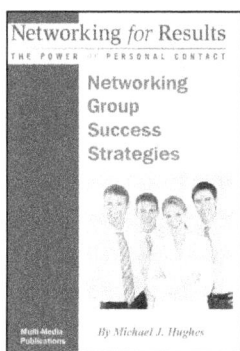

Networking *for* Results
THE POWER OF PERSONAL CONTACT

Networking Group Success Strategies

Multi-Media Publications

By Michael J. Hughes

The *Networking for Results* series of books, audiobooks, and DVDs shows us how to think about networking strategically, and gives us step-by-step techniques for helping ourselves and those around us achieve our goals. By following these best practices, we can greatly improve our personal networking effectiveness.

Visit **www.Networking-for-Results.com** for information on specific products in this series, to read free articles on networking skills, or to sign up for a free networking tips newsletter. Products are available from most book, ebook, and audiobook retailers, or directly from the publisher at **www.mmpubs.com.**

www.ingramcontent.com/pod-product-compliance
Lightning Source LLC
Chambersburg PA
CBHW060643210326
41520CB00010B/1723